To

From

Flavia

For information write Andrews and McMeel,
a Universal Press Syndicate Company,
4900 Main Street, Kansas City, Missouri 64112

ISBN: 0-8362-4701-9

THE SHARING
OF LOVE

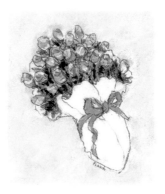

Written and Illustrated
by Flavia Weedn

The

sharing

of love...

FLAVIA

is the sharing

of promises and a

thousand little things.

It is

the making

of dreams

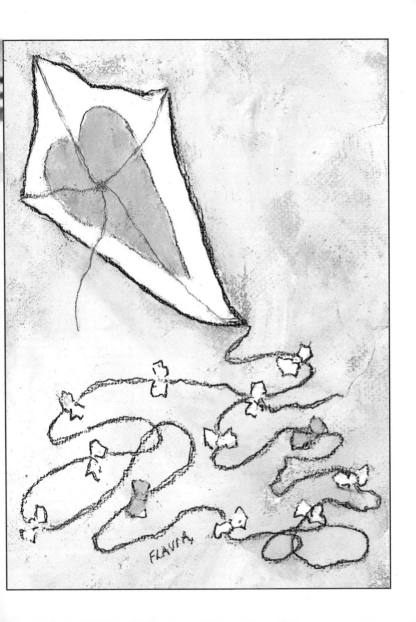

and

promises

to

keep.

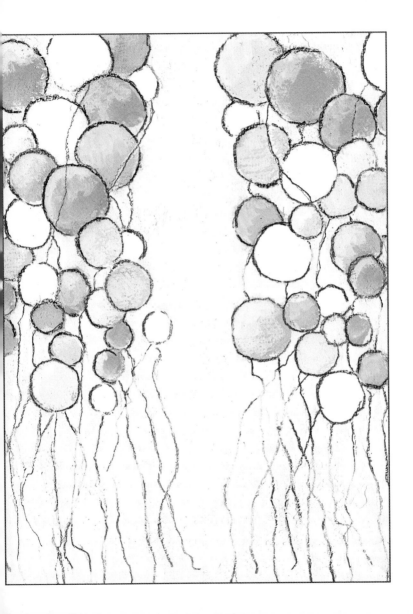

It is

having

stars

in your eyes

and

tomorrows

in your

heart.

It

is

the

giving

of songs

and of

silences

and

the

holding

of memories

only

the

heart

can see.

Sharing

a

lifetime

together

is

sharing

steps

in time.

FLAVIA

The music

is different

to each of us...

but

how

beautiful

the dance.

Flavia at work in her Santa Barbara studio

Flavia Weedn is a writer, painter and philosopher. Her life's work is about hope for the human spirit. "I want to reach people of all ages who have never been told, 'wait a minute, look around you. It's wonderful to be alive and every one of us matters. We can make a difference if we keep trying and never give up.'" It is Flavia's and her family's wish to awaken this spirit in each and every one of us. Flavia's messages are translated into many foreign languages on giftware, books and paper goods around the world.

To find out more about Flavia write to:
Weedn Studios, Ltd.
740 State Street, 3rd Floor
Santa Barbara, CA 93101 USA
or call: 805-564-6909